JOHN JOB

How can a man have knowledge of God?

LONDON

EPWORTH PRESS

FIRST PUBLISHED IN 1969
BY EPWORTH PRESS
Book Steward: Frank H. Cumbers
PRINTED IN GREAT BRITAIN
BY LAWRENCE BROS. (WESTON-SUPER-MARE) LTD.,
LONDON AND WESTON-SUPER-MARE
SBN 7162 0073 2

Foreword

The chapters which constitute the first part of this little book were originally lectures to a church membership class at Westminster College, Oxford. The Bible studies in the second part were written in response to a plea that it would be appropriate to include in any church membership manual an introductory course of readings, covering as far as might be possible, the skeleton of Christian doctrine. But they were used first as introductions to the readings in morning assembly at Rydal School. Each series occupied a week, and the course was spread at intervals over a year. Here, however, the Bible studies are intended to be complementary to the substance of the book, and if they are used again for school prayers, a series needs to be added on the Holy Spirit in the Church.

Ministers vary as to the length of the course which they conduct for new members. It is suggested either that the Bible studies are used privately by candidates concurrently with meetings to discuss the chapters; or that alternate meetings are devoted to dealing with questions which arise from the selections of Scripture passages.

J.B.J.

Rawdon

4 *December* 1968

PART ONE

1 What is the meaning of Baptism?

Here are Alan and Joan. They have both decided to join the Church. Alan's family have been faithful members ever since he can remember. They brought him when he was a baby to be baptized, and though he has been coming more or less regularly ever since, he wishes now to signify his personal acceptance of what was offered and promised then, and to profess publicly his allegiance to Christ and to the fellowship of Christians. Joan has only lately begun to come to services. She has not been baptized.

Becoming a member of the Church will involve for Joan being baptized. For Alan it will mean reminding himself of what was said and done at his baptism. It is right therefore that in thinking about Church membership we should begin with Baptism. Why was Alan baptized as a baby? Why is Joan to be baptized now? Jesus told his disciples to go into all the world, to teach all nations, *baptizing* them in the name of the Father and of the Son and of the Holy Spirit. This is a start; for it reminds us at the outset that Baptism is not something which man has invented. It is something instituted by Christ himself.

But what does Baptism mean?

1 It means becoming a member of the Church

If we look at the various instances of Christian Baptism recorded in the New Testament, we shall find that in every case a person's baptism marked the moment when he joined the company of Christians. For instance, on the day of Pentecost this is what distinguished those who accepted the Apostles' message from those who rejected it. This is how the Apostles knew who were joining their company; this is how the world at large knew who were becoming Christians: they were baptized.

Baptism, therefore, was for the New Testament Church what circumcision was for the people of God in the Old Testament. Just as in war-time every British citizen was given an identity card to distinguish him from aliens and entitle him to a ration-book, so circumcision was an outward sign distinguishing Abraham and his descendants (and also those who joined the clan) from the rest of the world.

This means that the act of Baptism effects a change of status. By living in a country for a certain length of time, a man qualifies to apply for naturalization. When he does so, his status is changed. Before, he was an alien. Now he is a citizen, with full rights to a vote and a passport. The New Testament teaches that the old national distinction between Israel and the Gentiles, circumcised and uncircumcised, is a picture of the distinction between the Church and the world —baptized and unbaptized. Baptism is that outward mark whereby Church and world may know who belongs to which.

So Alan, although in a sense he is only now joining the membership of the Church, in a sense became a member when he was baptized. It is important, as we shall see, to understand that becoming a member of the Church is not synonymous with becoming a Christian. Becoming a member of the Church is a change of status: it is something outward. Becoming a Christian is a change of nature: something inward.

But why was this particular sign chosen by Jesus? This brings us to a second answer to the question with which we started.

2 Baptism means 'washing'

The word 'baptize' comes from a Greek word which means *wash*. Thus John the Baptist invited men to come to the 'baptism of repentance for the remission of sins'. The act of baptism, this is to say, pointed to the washing away of the filth of sin. Dipping in the Jordan was a picture of this other deeper cleansing. John himself had no illusions about it. 'I baptize you', he said 'with water; but one mightier than I cometh . . . He shall baptize you with the Holy Spirit.' When the Syrian Naaman washed in the Jordan, the water washed him clean from his skin complaint. Naaman was also cleansed from the sin of pride. But it was not the water which washed this away. It was the Spirit of God working through the word of the prophet Elisha in his heart. The outward cleansing from leprosy was a picture of the inward cleansing from sin (see 2 Kings 5).

In the same way, Christian Baptism is an outward washing with water. In itself it entitles the person who is baptized to the earthly privileges of the Church. From this point he will be reckoned by the world as belonging to the Church, and from this point he will be welcomed into its fellowship as a member of the Christian family. But beyond this, the act of Baptism points to an inward washing by the Holy Spirit which cleanses from sin and gives to the believer that newness of life which Jesus promised. Baptism is not itself that inward washing. It is an illustration and symbol of it. When Ananias said to Paul, 'Arise and be baptized, calling on the name of the Lord', the act of Baptism was a visible token assuring him that God would hear his prayer and forgive his sins.

Christian Baptism is therefore an outward washing with water illustrating and symbolizing an inward cleansing which takes place when a man has faith in Christ.

But exactly what is this inward cleansing to which Baptism points? This brings us to a third answer to our question.

3 Baptism means identification with Christ

In order to understand this, we must look in rather more detail at the language which is used in the New Testament to

7

describe Baptism. We find not only the expression 'to be baptized with the Holy Spirit' to pinpoint the reality to which Baptism with water points, but also the phrase 'baptized into Jesus'. What does this mean? We get a clue from the Apostle Paul's first letter to the Corinthians, in which we read that the Israelites escaping from Egypt were baptized *into Moses* in the cloud and in the sea. This seems to imply that the Israelites were united with Moses in this experience: they were identified with him in it; they shared it with him. This helps to explain what Paul is saying in the other passage: 'Know ye not that so many of us as were baptized into Jesus Christ were baptized into his death? Therefore we are buried with him by baptism into death: that like as Christ was raised up from the dead by the glory of the Father, even so we also should walk in newness of life.' Jesus himself referred to his death as the baptism with which he would be baptized and said to some of his disciples that they would share this baptism with him. Almost certainly he meant by this that they would like him suffer violent death. But it is important to notice that Paul was talking to people who were in the ordinary sense still alive. Yet when he says, 'We were baptized into his death', and 'We are buried with him by baptism into death', he is obviously talking about an accomplished fact. If we were to ask Paul, then, what he meant by 'being baptized into' (or identified with) Christ, he would have replied as follows.

4 Baptism means dying and rising with Christ

However, this language is not self-explanatory, especially since Paul was not, as we have seen, talking about death in what we think of as the ordinary sense of the word.

Dying with Christ meant for Paul the end of a struggle to make himself acceptable to God. It meant admitting that he was helplessly and hopelessly involved in sin, and that he had utterly failed to keep the standard of God's law of love. It did not mean that he was physically dead, but it

8

meant that the old Saul who had persecuted the Church of Christ had come to a full stop that day on the Damascus road. It did not mean that from then on he was entirely sinless, but it meant that Satan was no longer king of his life. The slave who owed allegiance to that tyrant was dead. Whereas before this experience he was confined to a sinful orbit, revolving about himself, conversion released him from this confinement and planted within him the seed of a new life.

Paul speaks of this new life when he says of Christians that they are risen with Christ. The new link with Christ which is forged when a man becomes a Christian means also a new relationship with God. He calls him Father. The good things to which he now sets his hand are no longer attempted in his own strength to win God's favour, but in the strength which comes from gratitude that God's favour has been freely bestowed, that his failure to please God in the past is forgiven, and from the assurance that God's Spirit actually dwells in him when he trusts in Christ as a risen and living saviour.

Paul saw his baptism as a picture of this. The water with which he was washed spoke to him of the Spirit which both washed away his sin and bathed him with the power of the risen Christ to do God's will.

The objection may be made that if this is the meaning of Baptism, if it points to the deep truths of Christian experience, it can scarcely be appropriate to baptize infants, who are incapable of the faith which alone is the gateway to this new life. This is not the place for a full answer to this objection. But three points may be noted. (i) In all probability there were children in some of the whole households that were, according to the New Testament, baptized together, as for instance that of the Philippian jailer. (ii) This is the most convincing explanation of the fact that no controversy about baptizing infants arose in the earliest churches. If it were not taken for granted that whole households were baptized when the father became a Christian, we might expect this to have been a bone of contention from

9

the outset. (iii) Abraham's circumcision (like Christian Baptism) was a sign and seal of the righteousness which he had by faith. But in spite of the fact that circumcision had this spiritual significance, as Paul makes plain in his letter to the Romans, the ceremony was performed when a Jewish boy was eight days old. It thus anticipated (like Infant Baptism) the time when the child could understand its meaning.

What significance then has Baptism from the infant's point of view? Or rather, how are those who were baptized as infants to look upon their baptism?

5 Baptism is a sign and a seal of acceptance with God

In the first place there is no age limit on membership of the visible Church. There is doubtless a place for marking the moment when a person is prepared to declare his own acceptance of the promises made to him and for him at baptism. But to infer from this that baptized children are not proper members of the Church or that the Church is an exclusively adult society is a serious error.

Secondly, besides growing up with the knowledge that he is entitled to the outward privileges of Christ's Church, a child (or indeed an adult) may look back to his Baptism, if he is properly instructed, as a sign and seal of God's mercy and blessing. This may be, as it was for Martin Luther, a very real assurance in time of doubt. To baptize a child is to say to him, 'Christ died to blot out your sins, and is risen that you might have newness of life'. Of course, he could gather as much by reading the Bible. But Baptism confirms and applies personally the promises that are written there.

Here we may compare Baptism with marriage. The wedding ring is a sign and a seal of the husband's love. In giving his bride the ring, he means to give to her himself. And it is the promise of his love. In giving her the ring, he undertakes to support her for their entire future life on earth. So in Baptism God *covenants* himself to the child. He

10

offers the child himself. He promises his eternal love. On a note issued by the Bank of England are the words, 'I promise to pay the bearer on demand the sum of one pound', signed by the Chief Cashier. A child is given one: he does not understand these words or know what to do with it. But potentially he is richer. Similarly Baptism is a blank cheque drawn on the unsearchable riches of Christ.

Finally, therefore, Baptism constitutes a challenge. For just as the ring has to be accepted in marriage, and the husband's love reciprocated by his wife—just as the promise of the Chief Cashier has to be tested by trading with the bank-note—so too the fact that Baptism stands for a declaration, a promise, and an offer on the part of God means that there is a challenge to one who has been baptized. He must believe the declaration that Christ has died and risen again. He must test the promise that on the strength of this God will give to those who believe forgiveness of sin and newness of life. He must accept this offer. Christ has died to save this child: but will he come to the point of recognizing and hating his sin, so that these words become, instead of meaningless jargon, unspeakably precious? Christ has risen to give this child newness of life: but will he come to the point of seeing that in his own strength and by his own efforts he can never please God?

In a sense we take up this challenge when we become Christians, though not all can remember the day. In a sense we take it up when we publicly acknowledge our acceptance of Christ's promises in becoming 'officially' members of the Church. But in a sense it is a constant challenge. A bride does not rely on her husband's promise on her wedding-day alone, but hour by hour and day by day, enjoying an ever-deepening relationship. So too Christ's promises and Christ's offer, symbolized by Baptism, are a spring which never runs dry, and in responding daily to his love, Christians grow more and more to reflect his character until the day when they see him face to face in heaven and become altogether like him.

2 The Christian at home

'I appeal to you therefore, brethren, by the mercies of God, to present your bodies as a living sacrifice, holy and acceptable to God.' It has often been noticed that the crucial little word 'therefore' at this point in Paul's Letter to the Romans points in two directions. It points back to his explanation of what it means to be a Christian in terms of a healed relationship with God through Christ's death and resurrection. It points forward to the discussion, on which he is at this point about to embark, of various practical issues in the lives of those to whom he is writing: what it means to be a Christian in terms of everyday behaviour.

Baptism, as we have seen, is like this word 'therefore'. It points back to the death and resurrection of Christ and the meaning of these events for the believer, forward to the new life of the Christian. The Christian is called to translate 'dying and rising with Christ' into the vocabulary of words and deeds which the man in the street can understand. When Paul told the Philippians to *work out* their salvation, he chose a word to express this which can mean to turn bullion into coin. This is what the Christian must do with his faith. He must turn the great gold blocks of Christian doctrine into the currency of conduct.

Where is he to begin? When Jesus was about to ascend into heaven, he gave his disciples instructions to preach the Gospel in Jerusalem, and in all Judea and Samaria and to the end of the earth. Their witness was to begin where they were. When Andrew discovered that Jesus was the Messiah, he found his brother Simon and brought him to Jesus. Soon afterwards we find Simon introducing Jesus into his home to heal his mother-in-law. The Philippian jailer took Paul and Silas home when he became a Christian. Jesus even in the agony of the crucifixion did not forget his mother, but made provision for her to be looked after in coming days. The place for Christian witness to begin is at home.

12

At various stages one may be involved in any or all of three relationships: (i) with mother and father; (ii) with husband or wife; (iii) with children. About each of these three responsibilities there is important teaching in the Bible.

1 The relationship of child to parent

'Honour thy father and thy mother' is one of the Ten Commandments. The word for *honour* is a very strong one. It is used often for paying homage to God, and elsewhere only of the respect due to kings and other important people. It is important to bear in mind that the Ten Commandments are prefaced by the words, 'I am the Lord your God who brought you out of the land of Egypt, out of the house of bondage'. Similarly, where parallel teaching comes in Leviticus, we read, 'You shall be holy; for I the Lord your God am holy. Every one of you shall revere his mother and his father'. Again and again the point is made that the ethical standards commanded by God will distinguish his people from the Canaanites who had 'defiled the land'. In other words, from Moses onwards, respect for parents was a key feature of the witness of God's people to him.

So also in the New Testament, when Paul is outlining the character of the unbelieving pagan world, there comes in his list of their depravities the fact that they are disobedient to parents. One of the ways, therefore in which a Christian shows the reality of his faith is by the respect which he shows for his parents, as indeed Christ showed it for his (Luke 2 : 51). Paul reminds his readers in quoting this commandment that 'Honour thy father and thy mother' is the first with a promise attached to it: 'that it may be well with thee and thou mayest live long on the earth'. These things are added to those who seek first the kingdom of God and his righteousness.

Jesus himself quoted this commandment, and reinforced

13

its teaching together with another passage from the Old Testament which reads: 'He who speaks evil of father and mother shall surely die'. The temptation to criticize our parents often covers a desire to hide, perhaps even from ourselves, our own failings in the home. But the context is very important. Jesus is dealing with the evasion by the Pharisees of the law's insistence that a man ought to support his parents. The scribes maintained that if, maybe in a fit of anger, a man declared that he would give the money, otherwise to have been used for his parent's support, as an offering to God, he was bound by his oath to this effect. Jesus' point is that they are guilty of misinterpreting the Old Testament. By pressing to an absurd point its teaching about vows, they were capable of getting round any of the crucially important moral precepts. The point for us here is that honouring father and mother is for Jesus a crucially important moral precept. As for the suggestion that God should come first, even to the extent of depriving them of legitimate attention and support, this for Jesus smacks of the worst kind of hypocrisy. There are many modern situations in which this teaching is relevant. It is possible, for instance, to use Christian activity, or the work of the Church as a mask for indifference to parents' needs. It is possible to go abroad as a missionary to escape one's responsibility, or to refuse support to them in their old age on high-sounding moral pretexts. But those who do so fail to provide for their relatives are denounced by Paul as worse than unbelievers: 'they have denied the faith.'

2 The relationship of husband and wife

Just as honouring father and mother is represented by the Bible as part of the *witness* of God's people, so also is a right relationship between husband and wife. Most modern books on marriage give psychological reasons for the advice they offer. The Bible gives theological reasons. Modern books say in effect: 'You'll feel better if you do this and avoid that'. Paul says that marriage is a mystery ordained by God to illustrate the relationship between Christ and his Church. It follows therefore that a Christian man and wife have in their life together a vital sphere of witness, not merely in the way in which they open their home hospitably to others, though this is important; not merely in the way in which they bring up their children; but simply in their behaviour towards each other.

What is involved? Paul speaks first of the attitude of wife to husband, and then of husband to wife. 'Wives, be subject to your husbands as unto the Lord.' This teaching has been ridiculed largely because it has been misunderstood. The headship of the woman exercised by the Christian man is compared to the headship of the Church exercised by Christ. Christ's headship or leadership is not tyrannical. His yoke is easy and his burden is light. It is laid not externally on the shoulder, but inwardly on the heart. He rules not by force but by capturing the will. His service is perfect freedom.

This is why Paul goes on to say to husbands, 'Love your wives, even as Christ also loved the Church and gave himself for it'. Being head of the wife does not mean that the husband has an unchallenged right to the car and the camera. He exercises his authority not by taking, but by giving: lovingly and not selfishly.

Consideration of the way in which Christian marriage depicts the love of Christ and the Church is in itself enough to make clear that it should be out of the question for a Christian man or girl to marry an unbeliever. The unity of Christ and his Church is the unity of a vine with its branches, a man with his own body. But no such close link can bind one who accepts and one who rejects Christ. Paul says explicitly, 'Be ye not unequally yoked together with unbelievers. For what has righteousness in common with unrighteousness, or light with darkness?'

Paul had to deal with cases often enough where a man or a woman already married became a Christian, but not the partner. Usually the unbelieving husband would allow his wife to remain with him when she became a Christian. If so, she was not to seek for a divorce. It might be that by her tenderness and consideration she would win him for Christ. Sometimes she would find herself turned out of doors when she professed to be a Christian. In this case she was not to stand in her husband's way if he divorced her. She could not be sure that she would be able to convert him.

Though Jesus makes it clear that the Christian standard with regard to marriage and divorce is rigorous, he is arguing about what can be justified from a Christian point of view. What he says must not therefore be interpreted legalistically. No sexual misdemeanour (or indeed any crime) must be thought to exclude a person from becoming a Christian and joining the church (1 Corinthians 6: 9, 11).

Although the New Testament has little to say of relations between men and women before marriage, much of what is said about marriage is applicable. Peter, for instance, bids husbands live considerately with their wives, bestowing honour on the woman as the weaker sex, 'since', he says, 'you are joint heirs of the grace of life, in order that your prayers may not be hindered'. Here there are two principles, neither of which depends on whether the man and the woman are married. (i) From some points of view, woman is subject to man; but spiritually she is equal. 'It means', says Cranfield, 'that women are taken seriously as persons, and can no more be thought of, or treated, as mere drudges, mere child-bearing machines, or mere playthings.' (ii) Selfishness is a sure way of making it difficult to pray, because it is a sure way of erecting a barrier between us and God. Whether or not our relationship with God is enriched or impoverished is a reliable guide to how wisely we are conducting a friendship with someone of the opposite sex. Speaking to wives, Peter reminds them that their most precious adornment is the imperishable jewel of a gentle and quiet spirit rather than superficial finery of make-up and clothes. Does it mean no lipstick, no perms, no gold?

Peter would have been sad to think that his words would be interpreted as fashion-regulations to this effect. Nevertheless, the insistence that the beauty which is important is an inward spiritual quality, if addressed to wives, applies, if anything, even more strongly to girls before marriage.

It is sometimes thought that the New Testament represents marriage as a second-best. The grain of truth that this error embodies is perhaps best expressed by saying that in some situations, as for instance when physical persecution is imminent, or in some specific task to do with the spread of the Gospel, it may be wiser for a Christian not to marry. In no such circumstances, however, is it sinful to marry. Rather is it sinful not to marry, if abstaining is the source of strain and unconquered temptation. The fact that marriage is used by Paul to illustrate the union of Christ and his Church is enough in itself to show the high regard in which he held it. Nor must it be forgotten that it was at a wedding that Jesus performed his first miracle.

3 Children

It is obvious that in bringing up children in the home, there are alternative dangers of keeping them either on too tight or too loose a rein: of giving them a position of no significance in the family, or giving them such significance that they are bewildered and spoiled by the deference they are shown, and the decisions they are invited to take. The Christian doctrine steers a firm middle path between these errors. On the one hand, approval of the proverb, 'Train up a child in the way he should go' is evident in what the Writer to the Hebrews says of the manner in which God disciplines his genuine sons, thus proving that he is really their father. On the other, Jesus makes it plain in the incident when he has to rebuke his disciples for sending children away that they are not to be disregarded as though they were unimportant. The self-importance of grown-ups in putting children off prompted Jesus to point out to them that unassuming childlikeness was a qualification for the Kingdom of Heaven which they were in danger of missing. Self-importance is usually the fault if one treats children as if they were not there. A true Christian, therefore, who has lost this self-importance—and this after all is only putting in other words what is meant by dying and rising with Christ—will always be mindful of the receptive attitude of Jesus towards the young and the very young.

3   The Christian and the Church

The believer, as we have seen, has strict obligations to the human family to which he belongs. But as a believer, he now belongs to another family. 'My mother and my brothers', said Jesus, '—they are those who hear the word of God and act upon it.' It is clear too from these words that Christians owe to this spiritual family a greater allegiance than they owe each even to his own human family. This is not, as we have seen, to be used as an excuse for neglecting genuine obligations to the latter (cf. Mark 7:11); but on the other hand Jesus made it quite clear that the consequences of his coming would involve sharp divisions even between father and son, mother and daughter (Matthew 10: 34–38). The Christian is not called upon to bring about such divisions. On the contrary, it is his duty to heal them. But he is called upon to expect them, to bear with them, and not to cure them by abandoning the new spiritual allegiance which he has as a Christian.

Our task is now to sort out the obligations which a Christian has to this other family—the Church of Christ. Many of these obligations are clear from this very comparison of the Church to a family.

1   The household of faith

The most obvious duty of members of a family is to care for each other. If one member is ill, it is expected of other members that they will look after him; if he is financially in difficulty, to help him; if he is homeless, to provide for him. The duty of looking after fellow-members is equally pressing in the family of the Church. James makes no bones about it: 'Pure religion and undefiled is to visit orphans and widows in their affliction'. Why? Not, of course, because orphans and widows have any monopoly of the church's care, but because they are a striking example of the kind of people who need help—those who have no human family to which to turn. And so, though a Christian is bidden to do good, as he has opportunity, to all men, this becomes a special obligation towards those who are of the household of faith (Galatians 6: 10).

A further thought that springs from the idea that the Church is a family is this. Human families revolve very much round the needs of their youngest members. When a child is very young he monopolizes the attention of the older members of the family: not in the sentimental sense that they spend all their time admiring him, but in the severely practical sense that his needs limit and direct their activities. He needs to be fed and he needs to be looked after. It is a well known fact that children who do not receive proper care from their families are just the ones who, broadly speaking, become problems in their teens. The children in the family of the church also need proper care. It is a great mistake to imagine that the Church is an exclusively adult society. If we have a doctrine of infant baptism, we must carry it through to the logical conclusion that this marks the beginning of genuine membership. Children really do belong to the Church, just as much as they do to the home. We hear of the lapse of children from attendance at church during their teens. Might it not be that they have never been made to feel at home in the church? This means more than the casual affability of grown-ups towards them. It means the kind of interest in them which makes them feel at home *at home*. This responsibility is not carried only by Sunday School teachers or even only by adults. Older children play an enormous part in educating younger children in the home, and should be alive to the opportunities for drawing younger children into the fellowship of the church. The older boy or girl who, instead of being self-important, is welcoming towards younger children does a great deal to anchor them firmly within this fellowship. Furthermore one does not have to be a babe in arms to be a babe in Christ. What is true of those who are young in years is true also of those who are young in the faith, however old they are. The church must be geared to the needs of the immature as is the life of the home.

2 The body of Christ

The unity of the Church is emphasized in the New Testament by another picture of its relationship to Christ. Christ is not only the first-born of many brethren: he is 'the head of his body the Church'. This picture is used by Paul to teach various lessons.

In Romans 12, the apostle points out that the various members of the human body have each a particular function to perform. In the same way, so also have Christians as members of Christ's body. Twenty years ago, it used to be fashionable to declare various members of the human body useless: the tonsils and appendix for instance. More recently, the function of these organs in preventing disease has been discovered. Every member in Christ's body has a purpose; this is the message of the Parable of the Talents. The danger is, because I have been given a function that is less significant (at any rate to all appearances) than that of somebody else whom I know, to think that my part can be done without. Like the third man in the parable, we tend either from a false fear or a false shame, to pretend to ourselves or to others that God has not equipped us in any way for his service. It is not a matter of option whether we use our talent or not. To leave it unused is an offence of great gravity: the landlord, on his return, said, 'Cast ye the unprofitable servant into outer darkness'. So Paul in this passage bids each member perform his own task effectively and wholeheartedly. 'He that ruleth' comes next door to 'him that showeth mercy': the greatest and the least, in the world's eyes, are in the eyes of Christ, who is the head of the body, alike essential.

When Paul comes to argue from the same comparison of the church to the body of Christ in his first letter to the Corinthians, he makes the same point. Is the foot to say 'Because I am not a hand I do not belong to the body'? No; of course not. The foot and the hand have entirely different functions, and one is entirely unsuited to do the work of the other. So it is in the church. But Paul goes on from this point to combat the opposite extreme. The first extreme is to think that my task in the church is too insignificant to need doing properly. Its opposite is to think that my function in the church is the only one that matters. And so Paul says, 'The eye cannot say to the hand, "I have no need of thee"'. The eye is rated by insurance companies as the most valuable organ that one can lose. And yet, by itself, unaided by the executive team of hands, feet, mouth and voice, how ineffective it is. It is the mark of greatness in the church to recognize one's limitations. It is the mark of greatness in a minister, not that he is able to run the church by himself, but that he is able by God's help to discern the part to be played by those in his flock with the meanest equipment, and to evoke the faithful playing of it.

But this is not only the responsibility of the minister. The temptation to underrate or overrate one's own function in the church and the function of others is a temptation to which every single member is subject. How can we combat this temptation? Paul's answer is that in the human body each organ has a clearly defined purpose which no other organ can effectively fulfil: in the same way, a healthy church is one where the members recognize a similar pattern of interweaving responsibilities. It is in an understanding of how my part and his part and her part fit into the jig-saw, that the key to the united, harmonious, purposeful activity of the church lies.

The question arises: what am I to do when the church or its leaders adopt a policy with which I do not agree? Here we may look to the same picture of the Church as Christ's body for guidance. There are plenty of situations where a man takes a decision which, while it may bring benefit to him as an individual, or achieve his aim, is damaging to some part or other of his body. Yet his whole body is involved in such a decision. Similarly with a church. Its decisions are corporate. Every member is involved. Even if I do not agree, or if I feel that the policy is one which causes me personal hardship, I have a duty loyally to carry out that policy. The only case where I have leave to refuse is if I have firm scriptural grounds for thinking that in its declared policy, the church is running clean contrary to Christ's will and therefore no longer deserves to be called his body. Then, if I am right, it is no longer I who am guilty of schism, but those responsible for such a policy.

3 A more excellent way

When Paul had finished expounding the implications of this comparison between the church and a human body, he realized that there was something of supreme importance still to be said. 'I show you', he said, 'a more excellent way'. No matter how effectively a given part might be played— even if the preacher speaks with the tongues of angels, even if the prophet knows every mystery—there is something more important than the playing of parts in the church. Without it the most impressive efficiency is useless. And this thing is love. Other aspects of the church's life have a place only in time and space. But love has a place in heaven as well as on earth.

It is well known that those who translated the Old Testament into Greek, followed by the New Testament writers, chose to express their idea of love a word which was before of fairly uncommon usuage, and different from all the words which the Greeks had for human affection. The love which binds the Church together is not a love of human origin. There are fellow members of the Church to whom we feel naturally drawn, but there are many with whom from a merely human standpoint we might feel we have little in common. Why should we love them? And what does it mean? To answer this question, we are brought back to the point from which we started. The picture of the family and the picture of the body find their point of meeting in the person of Christ. We are a family because we are related to him, and through him to God. We are a body because we share a relationship to Christ who is the head of the body. But what is this relationship? It is the bond forged by the supreme act of love whereby Christ died for us while we were yet sinners. We love both him and our brethren in the Church because he first loved us.

4   The Christian and his work

Work is on the whole an unpopular institution. The Bible explains this fact as a consequence of man's sin, and the element of frustration which turns work into toil as part of the curse which Adam's disobedience called down upon his race (Genesis 3: 17–19). But the same story also implies that this was not God's original purpose. God put the man into the Garden of Eden to till it and keep it before he sinned (Genesis 2: 15). Throughout the Bible, moreover, the work of man is represented as a picture of the work of God, whether creative, administrative, or instructive: it is part of what is meant by man's being made in the image of God (Psalms 104: 23–24, Isaiah 28: 23–29). Sin has distorted, but it has not destroyed the image.

1   Overwork

Apart from the fact that work tends to be frustrating, there are various other ways in which man has turned what was originally and is in essence a blessing into a curse. The most important is the possibility that work may become an end in itself. Paul makes it clear that God's whole enterprise of creation had as its ultimate objective the salvation of man in Christ, and what is commended in man is not labour in itself, but the labour that springs from love.

There are two ways in which work may become an end in itself, and thus exclude the love which redeems it. Either it may become an instrument of greed, or it may become something in which one takes the wrong kind of pride. The Bible looks at both these things as idolatry. Greed is idolatry because it involves putting money in the place of God. The Bible draws attention to some of the results that this has upon work. In the sphere of industry, it leads to the underpayment of employees (James 5: 4). In the sphere of commerce, it leads to the kind of injustices that Amos speaks of when he addresses those who have made the ephah small and the shekel great—giving short measure to those who bought, but using heavy weights when it was their turn to buy. In the sphere of spiritual work, it leads to concentrating on the opportunity for financial reward rather than on the needs of those for whom one is responsible (Ezekiel 34: 1–5).

In all these cases the actual quality of the work suffers. But this is much less obviously so if we use our work as a means of bolstering not so much our bank-balance as our ego. Isaiah speaks of worshipping the works of men's hands as folly (Isaiah 44: 9–17). No doubt he was thinking of deliberate attempts to make gods. But the same principles apply when the achievements we are proud of are less tangible and become our gods without our realizing it. Am I a craftsman and proud of the things which I have made? They soon become objects of worship. Am I a businessman and proud of the organization whose wheels turn smoothly under my competent management? A teacher, and proud of the elegant writing or pictures or behaviour which my class produces? A minister, and proud of the big congregation or collection? In all these ways we make gods for ourselves because we shut God out. We take the credit which is solely due to him. The false gods of the Babylonians are the creations of the true God, Isaiah argues: he made the wood from which the image is carved. So also belongs to God the praise for all the things which we are proud of.

When our work is entirely concerned with things, there is a sense in which this kind of pride does not spoil it. For instance, a craftsman may be infuriatingly conceited about his work, yet we have to allow that his carpentry, or whatever it is, is flawless. But when our work is with people, it is impossible to keep separate the technical skill and the spiritual attitude with which we do it. There is something wrong with the class of the swollen-headed teacher, and much more with the congregation of the swollen-headed minister—especially if it really is he who is holding it together (1 Corinthians 3: 4–6).

2 The opposite extreme

So far, we have dealt with errors on the side of over-interest in work. There is also the opposite extreme. If work is frustrating for the sinner, he always has the simple expedient of avoiding it. But although the Bible recognizes the frustrations of work, it holds no brief for this method of coping with them. The commandment which bids us keep the Sabbath begins, 'Six days shalt thou labour' (Exodus 20: 9). And there are many proverbs along the lines of the one which says: 'An idle soul shall hunger' (Proverbs 19:15).

As Christians we are redeemed from the curse of the law. The law is a curse because we are unable in our own strength to keep it, and because it shows up our sinful nature for what it is. But with Christ's forgiveness for the past, and Christ's power for the future, the law that is for the unbeliever a curse becomes a blessing. For a Christian it is a lamp to his feet and a lantern to his path (Psalm 119: 105). So the commandment to work six days and rest on the seventh, is a curse for unbelievers (for some because they cannot bear to stop work, and for others because they cannot bear to start) but it is a blessing for Christians.

On one hand, those who have a tendency to overwork for financial reasons learn as Christians to trust a God who through Christ has shown himself to be their Father, to whom they pray, 'Give us this day our daily bread'; a God who sees a sparrow fall, who feeds the birds and clothes the grass of the field. They have heard Christ say, 'Are you not of much more value than these?' They have learned to seek first the kingdom of God, and his righteousness, and to trust the promise that all these things shall be added unto them (Matthew 6: 24–34).

Those with a tendency to overwork for the sake of priding themselves on their own achievements find in Paul a model of one who had such pride overturned when he yielded to Christ (Philippians 3: 4–11). 'Where is boasting?' he asks elsewhere (Romans 3: 27). 'It is excluded', he says. A Christian is one who has come to see that there is only one thing to be proud of, to boast about: the fact that Christ has died; not my achievement, but his.

However, deliverance from these motives for overwork is not meant to make a Christian idle. That Christianity itself was even in New Testament times made an excuse for idleness is clear from a number of references in Paul's epistles. There was a party in the church at Thessalonica, for instance, who, it seems, had given up work because they expected Christ's return to be so soon. Paul too saw the return of Christ as imminent. But the fact that this for him was only all the more reason for fulfilling earthly obligations shows how wrong it is to neglect the duties of our ordinary employment and human relationships on the pretext of supposed spiritual commitments (1 Thessalonians 4: 11). The other two passages point to the fact that idleness and mischief are never far removed from one another. For this reason, Paul advises Timothy to encourage younger widows to marry again (1 Timothy 5: 13), and he urges those who before they were Christians had lived dishonestly, stealing from others, to do an honest job which (by contrast with their former 'occupation') would provide them with something to give away to those in special need (Ephesians 4: 28).

Although the point of the passage in Ephesians is not that the ex-thief should do a *manual* job (since the expression 'with his own hands' simply means that he *himself* should do the work) manual labour is nothing to be ashamed of. Christ himself blessed this type of work no less certainly by growing up as the son of a carpenter than he blessed marriage by making a wedding the scene of his first miracle. Paul too, when he was in a situation where it would have been unwise or embarrassing to accept financial assistance for his services as a preacher, reverted to his trade as a leather-worker (Acts 18: 3). Not that he thought that preachers ought in principle to do this. Jesus said in this connexion, 'The labourer is worthy of his hire', and Paul, to prove the same point, interprets the words, 'Thou shalt not muzzle the mouth of the ox that treadeth out the corn' as relevant to the right of those engaged in spiritual work to expect financial help from those to whom they minister. But the teaching is of much wider application. The whole structure of society depends on the due reward of honest work. It is not for Christians to see that they get it, but it is for them to see that they give it, and that it is given to others.

3 Personal relationships

One final word must be said about relationships with other people involved in one's work. There is not much in the New Testament which refers specifically to this. But the same principles apply as are spoken of in a slightly different context. Slaves are told to obey their masters, and similarly employees have duties towards their employers and those whom their employers set over them. The important point to notice here is that it is not the character of the employer which decides whether the Christian in his service should respect him or not (1 Peter 2: 18). When he is ordered to do something which is clearly contrary to God's will, then he must disobey. But it is only too easy to resist those over us because we do not like them on the pretext that they are unjust. It is even easier to criticize them behind their backs, not because we have any real desire to set them to rights, but simply because human nature has an ingrained tendency to talk unkindly about those in authority. The power to conquer this comes from Christ, but it is a battle not easy to win in a day.

5 The Christian in the world

In his high-priestly prayer Jesus prayed that his disciples might preserve a delicate balance: they were to be in the world, but not of it (John 17: 14–17). Elsewhere this idea is expressed by picturing Christians as colonists or ambassadors. They exist where they do not belong. They live on earth, but their true citizenship is in heaven. Having dealt with the Christian's relationship with his home, his church, and his work, we have in his relationship with the world a further sphere in which his witness must be expressed. The teaching in the New Testament about this divides into two categories. On one side there is the emphasis on what the Christian must give the world; and on the other there is the emphasis on what the Christian must not take from the world: his duty to the world and the dangers of the world.

1 In the world

In the first place the Christian is a steward of the Gospel. That is to say, he has been *entrusted* by God with the good news about Jesus Christ. 'God so loved the world that he gave his only begotten Son, that whosoever believeth on him should not perish, but have everlasting life.' But this purpose is only fulfilled in so far as Christians make known to others the meaning of God's gift. Paul said he was under obligation both to Greeks and barbarians (or—as he goes on to explain it—to the wise and to the foolish). Like Paul, we are ambassadors for Christ, God making his appeal through us to all sorts of people. Like him we must proclaim both by what we do and by what we say, 'We beseech you on behalf of Christ, be reconciled to God'.

The world is at enmity with God, but the fault is not on God's side. It was man who made the original breach, and God has in the death of Christ made a standing offer of peace, of reconcilation. But how is this peace offer made known? It is made known through the witness of Christians. There is no indication in the New Testament that this witness should be confined to what one might call pulpit-preaching, though this is an instrument of evangelism which cannot be replaced. Every Christian must be on the alert all the time for opportunities of telling others about Christ.

This is not a suggestion that button-holing strangers is the way to make Christians of them. It simply means that when opportunities arise in conversation either with strangers or friends, we ought not to fight shy of them; we ought not to be ashamed of making clear where we stand, and where they could stand. Sometimes it may take five years to establish a relationship in which we can, without being rude, talk to somebody about spiritual issues. But sometimes it may take only five minutes. The woman at the well in Samaria was somebody in desperate need of spiritual help, and Jesus shows in his conversation with her how quickly the heart can be reached. He was bold, frank, uncompromising in his approach; but not rude (John 4).

We need to seek and pray for opportunities to give direct teaching by word of mouth to those around us. But a Christian's responsibilities to the world do not end here. Perhaps in a sense they do not begin here. But it is right to mention this direct evangelism first as something of crucial importance. If we waited until we were perfect before speaking to others about Christ, we should wait for ever.

Nevertheless Christians are commanded to be perfect. It may be something which will not be a reality this side of heaven, but there is all the difference between one who is striving and longing to be perfect and one who abandons the unequal struggle and sets his sights on some less exacting target.

Our relationship with the world provides us with some of the most difficult challenges that we face. Twice Paul speaks in his epistles of behaviour towards the world, or as he calls them, 'those without'. In Colossians 4: 5 he says, 'Conduct yourselves (walk) wisely toward outsiders', and in 1 Thessalonians 5: 12, 'Conduct yourselves with grace and dignity toward outsiders'. There is no doubt that here Paul is primarily thinking of behaviour in situations where the non-Christian knows that the person he is dealing with professes to be a Christian. Of course, involved in the running of a church there are inevitable dealings with outsiders. Indeed such dealings should not be avoided. The local grocer may sometimes have a just cause for complaint if the women's meeting dispenses with many of his services by questionable bring-and-buy sales. All the financial dealings of the church must be beyond reproach, and bills promptly paid. Anything one does as a representative of the Church should be done more rather than less conscientiously than what one does on one's own account. The aim should be to make the task of working for the church a pleasant prospect for any tradesman, not something that he dreads. Banker, printer, plumber, builder, undertaker—all are deadly arrows in Satan's quiver if they have just cause for complaint in our church.

The consideration and courtesy which we owe to non-Christians is not really owed to them in their own right, but to God. We are not to be men-pleasers, or content with what Paul calls eye-service: we are not, that is, to be content with the minimum that will show. Plenty of people, who are courteous enough on a pavement, are discourteous and selfish behind a steering wheel on the road.

It can only be that they are sad to be thought the worse of, until they become faceless, anonymous creatures, who, sixty seconds hence, will be a mile away, never to be seen again. Christians can never look at themselves like this; to do so is to offend their Father in heaven, whom they not so much fear to offend as long to please.

One further thing which concerns the Christian's being in the world: the fact that he is a citizen of a heavenly kingdom does not mean that there is anything unreal about his citizenship here on earth. Such obligations as are imposed by the state on its subjects are imposed also on Christians in it. Sometimes Christians mistakenly see their spiritual obligations as exempting them from their ordinary everyday duties. This is right when the state requires something contrary to God's will, but in a normal situation, to be a Christian should make one a more loyal citizen, a more reliable member of any body or society with which one is connected. He votes, pays rates and taxes, honours the Queen, is loyal to the government in power, whatever his political views.

2 But not of the world

The Christian therefore, we see, is in the world. There are things that he freely does for its benefit, there are obligations which it imposes and he accepts. But he is not *of* the world. The expression most frequently used in the New Testament to refer to Christians, without any reflection on their character as it was, though with far-reaching implications as to what it should be, is the word translated 'saint'. This word means primarily 'separated'. It implies on the one hand that Christians are separate from non-Christians; on the other, that they are identified with Christ. The separation involved, or sanctification (which simply means 'having-been-made-saints-ness') is not something that they do themselves, but something that the Spirit of God does in them (Romans 15: 16; 1 Peter 1: 2). The fact that it

31

is a spiritual distinction is very important: Christian sanctification is repeatedly differentiated in the New Testament from Pharisaism and asceticism. What is different about a Christian is not something superficial; it can never be defined by a catalogue of outward acts like going to Church, saying one's prayers, not drinking alcohol. It is something inward, or, as the Bible puts it, a matter of the heart. The motive of the Pharisee is to prove himself as good as, or better than, other men. The Christian's motive is to please God. The mistake of the ascetic is to think that parts of God's creation or all of it are unclean, impure. But the Christian believes that to the pure all things are pure.

Yet this does not mean that there ought not to be outward differences between Christians and non-Christians: it means simply that it is the inward spiritual difference that a Christian sets store by. He is not proud of it: he knows that it is something that God has done by his Spirit and not he by his goodness. But the very fact that something inward has taken place in the heart of a Christian cannot but express itself in his speech, in his acts, in the way he spends his time, and in a new sense of values. In all these ways he will be different from those around him, from those whose hearts are unchanged. Thus Peter writing to Christians says: 'Let the time that is past suffice for doing what the Gentiles like to do, living in licentiousness, passions, drunkenness, revels, carousing and lawless idolatry.' This demand is really based on a threefold change of attitude that should be evident in Christians. The desire for joy and security which a man looks for when he gets drunk is met in a deeper and more permanent way by the satisfaction which being a Christian gives. Loose sexual relations too are out of place in one who now looks upon marriage as a picture of the bond between Christ and his Church (Ephesians 5: 32), and fornication as a direct insult to Christ (1 Corinthians 6: 15ff.). So, thirdly, is idolatry, whether we think of it as worship of other gods, or whether in terms of self-worship and money-worship, which are the modern counterparts. If one asks whether it is wrong for a Christian to do this or that, the answer is yes if it is something like this which comes in the category of 'lawless'. If it is a more doubtful question, the answer would seem to be that a Christian ought not to be asking it in terms of 'Is it wrong?' Anything for which the best he can say is that it is not wrong is clearly a second-best for one whose alleged intention as a Christian is to please no longer himself but God.

3 Opposition

Finally, a word about opposition. 'They are surprised that you do not join them in the same wild profligacy', Peter says, 'and they abuse you'. Again and again in the New Testament there comes to Christians the warning that the world will hate and persecute them (John 15: 18–26). In this situation there are three grounds for comfort. Jesus himself was hated without a cause: we are sharing something that he bore. Secondly, because of this he is able to sympathize with us and uphold us. Thirdly, Jesus said: 'Blessed are you when men revile you and persecute you and utter all kinds of evil against you falsely on my account. Rejoice and be glad, for your reward is great in heaven for so men persecuted the prophets who were before you.' No Christian must seek persecution, but all must expect it, and pray that God will give them strength not merely to bear it, but rejoice in it.

6 The Christian's personal life

To be reminded of the various spheres in which a Christian's witness should be expressed is inevitably a challenge. 'Who is sufficient for these things?' we ask ourselves. Indeed, if it were not so, it would simply mean that we had set our sights too low. Jesus said to his disciples. 'Be ye perfect', and though no doubt these words were intended in part to prick the pride of anyone who might imagine that he had reached a pitch of conduct or character with which to be satisfied, they were meant too to give a Christian a goal towards which to aim. Not a goal to be reached on earth, but such that if a man does not strive and long for it on earth, he cannot truly call himself a Christian. For this reason the Christian life is compared to a battle and to a race. The question which arises is: 'Where does he get the armour in which to fight the battle; where does he get the energy with which to run the race?'

1 The nature of temptation

The whole conception of the Christian life as a battle prompts the question, 'Who or what is the enemy?' Many Christians would answer this by saying that it is ourselves who are the enemy. But it is important to see that to use language in this way is a concession to humanism which we cannot afford to make. If it is myself who am the enemy, surely the battle is already lost; the gates of the palace are open, the enemy sits on the throne. Who is there left to resist if I myself am the enemy? This is not a matter of words alone, it is the reason why so many Christians are the victims of their moods and feelings. Believing as they do that they themselves are the enemy, it is hard if not impossible for them to apply the Christian message to their situation. I wake up feeling un-Christlike. What can I do, but wait until I *feel* Christlike again? Or again, I commit sin. If it is myself that is ultimately responsible, what can I do but wait until I feel forgiven? Or, to put it in a nutshell, when it is 'myself' that is faithless and unbelieving, how can I have faith? This is the light in which we need to view St. Paul's description of the battle of faith. For him, the old self died at the moment when he became a Christian. From then on he could say, 'It is no longer I that live, but Christ that liveth in me.' This did not mean that his problems were over. He spoke also in two ways of temptation. In the first place he spoke of a devil or (as the word literally means) *slanderer*. The devil points his accusing finger at us and says 'sinful'. But as Christians we retort that through Christ's death, because we have been crucified with Christ, the sinful self is dead: the punishment that Satan claims has been paid. The life which I now live, at which he points his jealous finger, is not my life, but Christ's resurrection life at work in me; and this is as much beyond his harmful reach in me as it was in Jesus. This life is righteous. It is like a spring of pure water. If I am a Christian, this is my true self. However, in the second place, Satan is pictured by Paul as having an ally. This ally is sin, and Paul could say, 'We know that the law is spiritual; but I am carnal, sold under sin. I do not understand my own actions, for I do not do what I want, but I do the very thing that I hate. Now if I do what I do not want, I agree that the law is good. So then it is no longer I that do it, but sin which dwells within me.' But the point is that whether evil is pictured as the accuser outside, or as the tempter inside the camp, the enemy is never identified with the Christian's true self.

2   Christian armour

Once the enemy has been clearly seen, the Christian is in a far better position to fight. The purpose of his armour, as described by Paul in Ephesians 6, now becomes apparent. Since Satan's main weapon of attack is to cause the Christian to doubt the reality of his Christian life by accusing him of sin, much of the Christian's armour is to combat this threat. He girds his loins with truth; elsewhere Peter talks of Christians girding up their minds. The point is that though an intellectual grasp of the meaning of the Gospel is not in itself the *only* ingredient of salvation (the devil knows his Bible) it is an essential ingredient. The message of salvation is the word of truth. Christ claimed, 'I am the truth.' Christian doctrine may be expressed as a series of propositions. Ultimately these propositions are painting a picture of Christ. But before we can ever begin to have true faith, we must know what these propositions are. We need to have seen the person of Christ. So important is this that Paul makes it the foundation of the Christian's armour. A Christian needs to know what he believes; the source of this knowledge is the Bible. These, says Jesus of the Old Testament Scriptures, are they which testify of me. There is no way of increasing our knowledge and grasp of Christ which replaces intimacy with God's word. Understanding the truth is the beginning of a Christian's spiritual life. It is also the highroad to growth in grace. It is the pure milk given to babes in Christ. It is the first step in the Christian's preparation for action—to gird his loins with truth. In practical terms there is no substitute for regular Bible-reading.

How does this Bible-study help us in time of doubt? Paul goes on to speak of the breastplate of righteousness. The breastplate is that piece of armour which enables one to face the enemy. Jesus himself provides us with an object-lesson in his temptation in the wilderness. He knew God's will for him because he knew God's word. He confronted Satan with obedience to that word, with an impenetrable breastplate of righteousness. Satan's main aim with Jesus was to make him disobey. His main aim with Christians is to sadden them by contemplating their own failure to obey God, their own unrighteousness. It is here that the Christian needs a knowledge of Scripture, to remind him that the very fact of being a Christian can be summed up in his admission of guilt—('if we say we have no sin we deceive ourselves')—and his reliance therefore not on his own righteousness but on Christ's. 'You are a sinner', says Satan. But God has forgiven my sin. My breastplate may be full of holes, but God has given me a new one: the one which I wear now is the one which stood up to Satan's attacks in the wilderness, and will stand up to them for ever. Christ relied on his perfect obedience. We rely on God's promise to forgive us. We trust not in our obedience but

Christ's. Paradoxically, this act of trust enables us ourselves to obey God.

The sandals, about which Paul now goes on to speak, are a reminder of the alacrity with which one will go to deliver a message of good news. But here again, the readiness springs from an understanding of the good news. What prompts a Christian to speak to others of it is a firm grasp of the benefits which the message has brought to himself, and an assurance that the same message will meet their needs. The peace of God which he preaches to others must be a real part of his own experience. A Christian who is doubtful whether Christ really has cancelled his sins and imparted new life to him will not be in the same position to commend this to others as one who is sure. Peter spoke boldly on the day of Pentecost because he was sure that Christ had risen from the dead, because he was sure that this meant forgiveness for him. But how can one increase one's assurance? By regular reading and meditation on the Bible. It is as one sees Christ as the consummation of God's purpose in the history there recorded, that one's doubts about his person, his teaching, his reality vanish.

It is only after this preparation that Paul mentions faith. So far he has stressed that in combating Satan the Christian must have something to believe. Now the point is that he must believe it. But surely it is just here that the problem arises, since the fiery darts of the evil one are aimed to undermine our belief. The answer to this is that our strength is not the firmness of our grasp of the shield, but the strength of Christ who is himself the shield. When Peter took his eyes off Jesus, he began to sink; but his trembling, uncertain 'Lord, save me' met with immediate response. It was not the assurance with which he made the request, it was the sureness of the one to whom he turned. To take the shield of faith is to remember Christ's reliability; in depression, to remember the hope that he has given us; in doubt, to remember his promises; in difficulty, his unconquerable resources; in pride, his humility; in temptation to sin, to remind ourselves that he died to purchase us from its power, that we are dead to sin, crucified with him, bought with a price and no longer our own.

The Christian's helmet is said to be salvation. A head-wound is dangerous beyond one to any other part of the body. The last enemy Paul calls death, and the last piece of defensive armour which he mentions here is the one which deals specifically with it. Death is something which is mentioned little because it is feared much. Fear of death wreaks havoc in people's lives. Not only does it trouble those who have no knowledge of Christ, but it fills with apprehension many who have. Yet this helmet of salvation is available for every Christian; the hope of a promised land to which, far from being able to exclude us, death merely opens the door. For as with Christ himself, the Cross turned out to be the highroad to glory, so with those who trust him, death is but a step towards the resurrection which we shall share with him.

Most of the Christian armour is defensive. In so far as our Christian life is a battle, it is a battle with an enemy who is himself often on the attack. Nevertheless there is in the sword of the Spirit a weapon with which the Christian may carry the war into the enemy's camp. This is the word of God. We are often in the position of being able to strike a blow for the extension of Christ's Kingdom by what we say in conversation.

There are two extremes which we must avoid. One is the thought that our own ideas, our own arguments are the weapons we should employ for this purpose. It is tempting to substitute what we think are good reasons for becoming a Christian for the arguments in the Bible. It is tempting to draw a picture of what it means to be a Christian from our own experience rather than one based on the New Testament. Not that there is any need for conflict here.

The other extreme is to imagine in our anxiety to do justice to Scripture that the people to whom we are endeavouring to present the Gospel are like juke-boxes; and that all we need to do is to plug in the right text and they will play the right tune. People are people and not machines. They do not respond automatically to technical data, however correct, but to a message which they understand. To wield this sword of the Spirit, one must have the ability not merely to quote appositely but to explain sympathetically the Word of God.

3 The place of prayer

Paul ends his description of the Christian armour with a command to master it through prayer. It is true that his panoply, as we have seen, depends largely on a book. But the Christian does not worship the book. The book is about a person, a living God. Without his help and the enlightenment of his spirit, the book is meaningless to us. For if he does not guide and support us, we cannot begin to follow or obey him. Furthermore no amount of human intellect will enable a man even to understand the Bible without assistance from God. Therefore he must pray: he must ask God for help, both to see and to do his will.

But the Christian battle is not something that concerns ourselves alone, as though each believer were engaged in single combat with Satan. Again and again the New Testament reminds us that there is a fellowship. We serve together and we suffer together. Prayer, therefore, says Paul, is not simply to be made to strengthen the individual, it is to be made for 'all the saints'. He reminds the Ephesians of his own chains and of his own responsibility in the task of spreading God's word. So every Christian remembers not only, or first, to pray, 'Give us this day our daily bread', but 'Thy kingdom come', recalling before God the difficulties and the opportunities of those whom he himself knows, commending to him the battle as a whole as well as his own particular outpost.

7 Holy Communion

A man is born once, but is fed often. Baptism, as we saw at the beginning, is a picture of the beginning of the Christian life. Like birth, Baptism happens once. Baptism reminds us of Christ's saying, 'I am the door'. Holy Communion reminds us of Christ's saying, 'I am the bread of life'. Because Christ died and rose again we can become Christians. Because Christ died and rose again we can live as Christians, and it is our *continuing* dependence on Christ's death and resurrection that is the meaning of our *regularly* attending the sacrament of our Lord's Supper.

It is helpful to compare these two sacraments which Jesus instituted. For rightly to understand one is rightly to understand the other. Just as in the case of Baptism washing with water is only a symbol of the inward cleansing from sin effected by the Holy Spirit, so in the case of Holy Communion the eating of bread and the drinking of wine are a symbol of appropriating by faith the benefits of Christ's death. It goes without saying that the word of God needs to be understood when it is preached. But in the sacraments the word of God is being dramatized, and it still needs to be understood. Merely to receive the elements at Holy Communion is the same as merely to hear the word of God. The only people who receive Christ at Holy Communion are those who, in taking the bread and the wine, realize 'the benefits which by his precious blood-shedding Christ hath obtained for us'.

1 The elements

When the elements are consecrated, the formula instituted by Christ is the same as when he said grace before a meal. None of the Gospels says that Jesus blessed the food,[1] as though this 'did something to it'. At the service of

[1]The A.V., it is true, has the expression 'and blessed it' (Matthew 26: 26), but the object is not expressed in the Greek text. The reason why the word 'bless' is used is because the Jewish grace began 'Blessed art *thou* . . .'. Luke, writing with a Gentile readership in mind, used the unambiguous expression 'gave thanks'.

Holy Communion the elements are not changed: they are simply put to a special use. In particular, they are not changed into the body and blood of Christ. To fall into this error is to be liable to make two further mistakes. The first is to imagine that Holy Communion is the sacrifice of a sin-offering to God and that Christ is the victim who 'dies again' on each occasion. We do not offer the bread and the wine to God: we receive it from him. We are not *making* a sacrifice (except in the sense that we offer ourselves for his service as a thank-offering): we are *remembering* the sacrifice of Christ once offered. We can test our motives by asking ourselves the question: are we coming to Holy Communion to confer a favour on God, or to acknowledge our need of his favour to us? The second mistake is to regard the minister as a priest, in the Old Testament sense of the word, who performs this sacrifice on behalf of the people. The truth is that, if he is truly preaching God's word and if he is rightly administering the sacraments, the minister is not offering to God anything in the name of the people except that he voices their praise and prayers; he is in the name of God offering the benefits of Christ's death and resurrection to the congregation.

Just as, in the case of Baptism, we had to ask the question, 'Why was this particular sign chosen?' so here we ask, 'Why bread and wine?'

a. The bread

The bread, as we have seen, stands for Christ's body. To eat it symbolizes one's acceptance of the living power made available through his resurrection. Just as I depend on bread (that is, food in general) for physical energy, so I acknowledge that the risen Christ is the source of spiritual energy.

But before the bread is distributed, it is broken. Christ lives in the hearts of believers through his spirit because He has risen from the dead. But he could not have risen from the dead without first having been crucified. In order to illustrate this, Jesus explained the necessity of his death and resurrection by comparing it to the need for a grain of wheat to perish in order for the harvest to grow. The breaking of the body of Christ meant death upon the cross to him, but life to those who come to understand and accept the benefits of that death. And it is just this which taking the bread at Holy Communion symbolizes: 'I take and eat this in remembrance that Christ died for me and feed on him in my heart with thanksgiving'.

b. The wine

The wine stands for Christ's blood. The bread and the wine do not symbolize exactly the same thing. Whereas bread is a symbol of nourishment, wine is a symbol of the joy that results from a restored relationship. We are fed by the body of Christ, but we are washed by his blood. The word 'blood' is used in the Bible as evidence of the death of a victim. To drink a person's blood is a vivid way of expressing the idea of reaping benefits from his death. The question then is, what benefits does a man reap from the death of Christ? And the answer reiterated again and again in the New Testament is that through the death of Christ a repentant sinner is pardoned. The sinner deserves to die, but Christ died, who did not deserve to die. We have sinned, but Christ bore the penalty. 'The chastisement of our peace was upon him [that is, the punishment whereby our communion with God was restored was borne by him] and by his stripes we are healed.' For Christ the cross was a bitter cup, because he suffered estrangement from God: He was made a curse for us. But the cup of his blood is for this reason the 'cup of blessing' for those who trust him, because, being the evidence of Christ's death, it is evidence that we are forgiven.

2   Holy Communion is the Christian Passover

It is no accident that Jesus instituted the sacrament of Holy Communion at the Jewish feast of Passover, for he meant this remembrance of his death to be its replacement and fulfilment. The point of the feast of the Passover was to remember the day when God rescued his people from Egypt. And it was almost certainly a deliberate reference to this when Christ said of the bread and the wine, 'Do this in *remembrance* of me'. In Christ's eyes, the redemption from Egypt was a concrete picture of the redemption from sin effected by his victory on the cross. In the same way Paul speaks of Christ as our Paschal Lamb (that is a lamb sacrificed for the Passover feast). There are various important consequences of the fact that for the Christian the sacrament of the Lord's Supper takes the place given by the Jew to the feast of the Passover.

a.   Passover was essentially a family feast

The feast of the Passover bound Jews together as the distinctive people of God, and this is true too of the Lord's Supper for Christians. By keeping the feast they remind the world outside of their allegiance to Christ, and they remind themselves that it is this common loyalty to Christ which gives unity to the spiritual family of the Church. The father's duty as host at the feast of the Passover was to interpret the various parts of the meal. Jesus himself probably did so at the Last Supper adding what is recorded in the Gospels as the institution of the new sacrament. He was the host then, and wherever his people gather to keep the feast, he is the host now; just as when he went in to eat with the two disciples at Emmaus, it was Jesus that broke the bread. He is the head of his body the Church. We invite him to join us. But he comes to the feast not as guest but as host.

b. *Passover was a covenant-meal*

Eating together is the outward expression of the inward bond of family affection. In Biblical times this symbol was of greater significance than it is today. Those who ate together were in covenant relation with each other. They were bound together with ties comparable to those which bound the family together. These ties were originally expressed by the slaying of a sacrificial victim, probably signifying that the two parties invoked upon themselves the fate of the animal if they broke the well-understood terms of family loyalty. The Old Testament records how God himself made a covenant in this way with Abraham, and the account of the covenant with the people of Israel at Sinai also contains the killing of a sacrificial victim, and the sprinkling of its blood over the people. When therefore Jesus said as he took the cup, 'This is my blood of the covenant which is shed for many', he was impressing on his disciples that the family relationship between the people of Israel and their God in the past was a picture of the new family relationship whereby Christians call God 'Father' and their fellow-believers 'brothers'. The breaking down of the barrier which divides the sinner from God breaks down the barrier which divides man from man.

Every covenant had implications for the past, for the present and for the future, and these implications are shared by the New Covenant between Christ and the Church, and hence too by the sacrament by which that covenant is reaffirmed in the service of Holy Communion.

I FORGIVENESS FOR THE PAST

To make a covenant with a man was to end hostilities with him. As we drink the cup in memory of the New Covenant, we remember that 'God was in Christ reconciling the world unto himself'. This then is the point of the Comfortable Words. Whatever sins we have committed, the wine is a token, which we can see, that we have 'an

44

advocate with the Father, Jesus Christ the righteous, and that he is the propitiation for our sins'. We may feel: 'God is angry because of my sins', but as we are reminded of the meaning of the death of Christ, we realize that God has taken the initiative himself to blot out the sins which caused his anger.

But those who come appropriating in this way the benefits of Christ's death only do so truly if they at the same time forgive others. The wicked servant is condemned in the parable because, though forgiven a huge debt by his master, he refused to let off his fellow servant a trifling sum. Knowing that God has forgiven us is what makes us able to forgive our neighbours, for there is no way of understanding God's forgiveness unless we are also grateful; and such gratitude is the essence of a forgiving spirit.

II PEACE FOR THE PRESENT

The death of Christ happened a long time ago—or so it seems to twentieth-century man. It is hard to see our peace with God sealed by something apparently so remote. Because the Eucharist happens now, and because its symbolism is so personal, it is specially suited to be a powerful means of assurance. Because all that we have done in the past to spoil our relationship with God has been blotted out and forgiven, we enjoy now an unbroken relationship with him. To know that this is so—that there are now no barriers, no clouds, nothing between us and God—to know this is the greatest blessing that this life affords. To help us to have this certainty is the purpose for which this sacrament has been instituted by Jesus. We must pray that this purpose will be fulfilled for us when we come to the service. It does not mean that we ignore sin: Paul bids every man examine himself, realize what he has done amiss, and turn from it—if necessary, making amends to those whom we have wronged, before eating of the bread and drinking of the cup. But complacency in sin and assurance of forgiveness from sin are very different things: the one is the greatest bane and the other the greatest blessing of the Christian life.

III HOPE FOR THE FUTURE

The word by which the New Testament writers represented the Hebrew word for *'covenant'* was the ordinary expression for a will. This is how the word 'covenant' comes to have the meaning which we most naturally associate with it—a solemn promise. The covenants which God made in the Old Testament, especially the covenants with Abraham and David, were, besides establishing a new relationship, solemn promises by God concerning the future. Abraham's descendants, for instance, were to possess the land of Canaan. By the New Covenant, sealed by the blood of Christ, God makes Christians his heirs—fellow-heirs with Christ of a heavenly kingdom. Jesus left his disciples with the title deeds, as it were, of this inheritance—a meal. For those who participate with a true understanding of its meaning, this meal is a guarantee of our place at the table in heaven. Christ met with his disciples at the Last Supper. He meets with them when they gather in his name to remember him. But the true banquet—true union with Christ—unhindered by the limitations of flesh and blood—awaits the day when we shall see him face to face in his Father's House.

> My Jesus to know
> And feel his blood flow
> 'Tis life everlasting, 'tis heaven below.
> Yet onward I haste
> To the heavenly feast:
> That, that is the fullness, but this is the taste.

PART TWO

1 How can a man have knowledge of God?

1 The Revelation of God in nature

When the Apostle Paul was presenting the message of Christianity to those who were unfamiliar with the Jewish faith, he took as his starting point the created universe. Here in nature is the way in which God reveals himself universally to all men. In Psalm 8, the poet expresses his wonder at God's concern with man in view of the magnificence of creation, and in Psalm 19, the heavens are said to 'shout' their silent word of witness to God's handiwork.

Psalms 8, 19.

2 The Revelation of God in history

It is the belief of the writers of the Bible that God is revealed in the whole course of human history; but more fully and particularly in the history of the nation of Israel. In Psalm 105, the writer bids his people share with other nations the revelation of God committed to them through their own national history. Their failure through sin to respond to this call set the scene for the climax of God's revelation of himself in history—the coming of Christ.

Psalm 105.

3 The Revelation of God in Jesus Christ (i)

Although God is revealed in nature and history, this is only a partial revelation unless one includes as its crown the entry of God into nature and history as the man Christ Jesus. The Father's supreme activity in nature is the giving of life; his supreme activity in history is judgement. Both these functions are combined in Christ his Son.

John 5: 19–29.

4 The Revelation of God in Jesus Christ (ii)

Jesus claimed a uniquely intimate relationship with God the Father. How is this claim substantiated? He speaks of three lines of evidence. First, there was the witness of John the Baptist, whom the Jews recognized as a true prophet. Then there were the things Jesus did, through which the Father himself directly confirmed his claim. Finally there was the evidence of the Old Testament.

John 5: 30–47.

5 The Revelation of God in the Bible

God's revelation in nature needs to be interpreted, and his revelation in history (particularly in the coming of Christ) needs to be recorded, in order to be available to more than the relatively small number of men who were eye-witnesses. The claim of the New Testament to provide accurate eye-witness accounts of the life and teaching, the death and resurrection of Christ is the most important aspect of the wider claim that the Bible as a whole is a reliable record and interpretation of God's revelation.

Luke 1: 1–4; 1 John 1: 1–5.

6 Revelation of God in the lives of other people

When King Herod saw the effects of the disciples' mission, his immediate reaction was to make a comment not about them but about Christ, whose power he recognized in their work. Paul makes the claim when writing to the Corinthians that it is as though God were making an appeal to them through him. But it may be quite unwittingly that people are used to speak to those for whom he has a message.

Mark 6: 7–16; 2 Corinthians 5: 14—6: 2; Matthew 25: 31–46.

2 The mystery of wrong

1 The origin of evil

In the Bible's narrative, the creation of man is quickly

followed by the entry of evil into his heart. This story teaches two important truths. First, sin is something more than spontaneous disobedience to God on the part of man. Second, however, man cannot shift the blame for it on to the force of evil which invades and leads him astray. No explanation is given either here or anywhere else in the Bible of how or why evil entered a world which God pronounced 'very good'.

Genesis 3: 1–13.

2 Is God responsible?

Pain, suffering and temptation all have a positive part to play in the making and perfecting of a Christian. Yet, having said this, James, in this passage for study, goes on to say that a person who is tempted must not make the mistake of thinking that God is responsible. For human reason, these two truths are impossible to reconcile. But the Bible presents them side by side, to be reconciled in experience.

James 1: 2–4, 12–18.

3 Is God in control?

There seems to be no rhyme or reason about the way in which pain and suffering are apportioned, and there is a temptation for those who trust God to wonder whether it pays. This was exactly the feeling of the writer of Psalm 73. At the end, he can still see no logical reason why the ungodly should prosper, but he has found in communion with God a source of comfort which puts the problem in a completely different light.

Psalm 73.

4 What is sin?

Although the Bible does not explain how sin and evil arose, and leaves many questions about them unanswered, it makes quite clear what sin is. The fundamental definition of sin is dishonouring God. It is often described therefore as rebellion against him, falling short of his standard, or as idolatry. A number of passages like this one from Jeremiah could be found, where these three descriptions are brought together.

Jeremiah 2: 5–8, 26–32.

5 Sin and others

Sin is basically dishonouring God. But it never stops there. Dishonour to God is always reflected in wrong behaviour towards other people. Paul expresses this very strongly in a passage at the beginning of his letter to the Romans. It is part of God's judgement upon sin that those who have a wrong attitude to God cannot avoid treating others in a way which they know very well is wrong.

Romans 1: 18–32.

6 Sin and self

Just as sin involves a wrong view of God, and a wrong attitude to other people, so too it involves a wrong attitude towards oneself. The parable of the Rich Fool and the parable of the Pharisee in the Temple paint pictures of two types of unbeliever. In some ways they are very different: one studiously neglectful and the other studiously attentive where religion was concerned. Notice, however, in both, the tell-tale incidence of the word 'I'. They were both men who put themselves in the place of God.

Luke 12: 13–21; 18: 9–14.

3 The Incarnation

1 The Fact of the Incarnation

The thing which distinguishes Christianity from other religions is not the moral standard which it sets before men, but the way in which it claims that God has dealt with man's failure to reach that standard. What was this method? It is summed up in the words 'God became man'. This is the doctrine of the Incarnation, so called from the Latin word for *flesh*. Here at the beginning of John's Gospel we find the verse which explains the origin of this term. The word *flesh* in the New Testament means 'ordinary human nature'.

John 1: 1–18.

2 The Reason for the Incarnation

The questions 'Who is Jesus?' and 'What has Jesus done?' are closely connected. He is able to offer the kind of remedy that he has provided only because of the kind of person that he is. Here, the writer to the Hebrews takes it for granted that such a remedy must come from God. He seeks to explain why it was fitting for the instrument through whom he worked to be genuinely human.

Hebrews 2: 8–18.

3 The Nature of the Incarnation

Although there is no attempt to explain fully how the Incarnation became possible, it is important to notice that the New Testament writers stated their teaching about the person of Christ in such a way as to refute two wrong theories about him. One is that Jesus was a divine being who only appeared to be a man outwardly. The other is that he was really a man, but because of his outstanding qualities was adopted by God as his son. Paul here guards against both these errors.

Philippians 2: 5–11.

4 Jesus' Baptism

The divine message heard by Jesus at his baptism is a combination of two Old Testament quotations. One is from a psalm which conferred God's authority on the Messiah. The other is from Isaiah, where God's servant is described as a human being who endured suffering and death. When Jesus, by undergoing baptism, identified himself with those whom he had come to help, he received this assurance that

51

he had set his feet on the way which would weave together the fulfilment of two apparently contradictory prophecies.

Matthew 3: 13–17.

5 Jesus' Temptation

The ministry of Jesus began and ended with prayer battles. Nor were they by any means the only recorded occasions when he engaged in long periods of prayer. Here too we find the mystery of the Incarnation unfolding: completely at one with God, Jesus was yet completely dependent on God. The reality of his temptation in the wilderness and of the agony in Gethsemane underline the genuineness of his human nature, while the victory which he won was a mark of his divine character.

Luke 4: 1–13; 22: 39–46.

6 Jesus' Transfiguration

Though the disciples came to recognize Jesus as the Son of God, they were bewildered by his telling them of his coming death. How were they to see beneath the defeated figure on the cross the victorious figure of the King of Heaven? This is the question which the Transfiguration was meant to answer. The divine message was the same as at Jesus' baptism. This time, however, it was addressed to the disciples.

Matthew 16: 24—17: 8.

4 The Ministry of Jesus

1 The Preacher

The Jews expected the Messiah to be a warrior king. This was a picture of his task which Jesus rejected. But how did he see the work that he had come to do? The readings in this section are chosen to illustrate from Jesus' ministry the various ways in which he understood what he was doing. He began where John the Baptist left off. Jesus said of *him* that he was more than a prophet; and Jesus himself, of course, was much more than a prophet. But this is where he started; and from the synagogue at Nazareth to the upper room, Jesus was a preacher. His message, gradually unfolding up to the threshold of Calvary, was that though the world was at present in the hands of the power of evil, the rightful kingship of God was in himself to be restored.

Matthew 4: 12–25.

2 The Lawgiver

To those who responded to his proclamation of God's kingship, Jesus gave a new law, which is summarized by Matthew in the Sermon on the Mount. In fact the Sermon on the Mount is not so much a new law (for almost all its teaching is found somewhere in the Old Testament), but the demand that the law should be looked at in a new way: those who saw in it only a line not to be crossed had already crossed it; Jesus taught his disciples to see, beyond this, guiding principles for the expression of Christian love.

Matthew 5: 13–20.

3 The Ruler

Jesus was not only the herald of God's kingdom, and its lawgiver: he was also, and is, its king. The words put by Pilate over his cross, 'The King of the Jews', intended to mock him, were profoundly true. Jesus, however, avoided for the most part the title 'Messiah', preferring to call himself 'the Son of Man'. This phrase was taken from the Book of Daniel, where it describes the representative of God's people, who, after defeat by their enemies, received power and dominion from God. Jesus, in this passage, explained to his disciples that this is what will happen to him.

Luke 9: 18–27.

4 The Servant

Jesus understood his work as the Son of Man in the light

of another Old Testament figure, the suffering servant of God, described in four poems embedded in the text of Isaiah (42: 1–7; 49: 1–9a; 50: 4–11; 52: 13—53: 12). It is hard to tell whether this prophecy originally referred to an individual or to a small godly group within an Israel which had become corrupt. But, though it has been disputed, there is strong evidence that Jesus saw himself as fulfilling in his ministry the role of this servant of God.

Luke 22: 24–37; John 13: 1–11.

5 The Deliverer

Jesus understood his task as God's servant as that of releasing men from the prison of sin. At his baptism, he identified himself with those whom he had come to save, and on the cross he finally defeated the powers of evil by which they were bound. But his whole ministry, seen as a conflict with sin and evil in every form, was an anticipation and an illustration of this final victory.

Mark 4: 35–41.

6 The Revealer of God

In his ministry, Jesus is seen as fulfilling various roles: he is at once the herald, the lawgiver, and the king of the Kingdom of God. He is God's chosen, whose task is to rescue from the power of evil sinful men. But he is more than God's agent. He claims to reveal God in such a way that anyone who has seen him has seen God himself.

John 14: 1–11.

5   The Cross

1 Revelation

The whole of Jesus' ministry was a revelation of God. But this revelation came to its climax in his death. There are various angles from which we may seek to understand the

54

cross, and this will be the theme of the readings in this section. But the view we get from these other angles will only be free from distortion if we remember this. In the love, which Jesus showed at his death, for his enemies and faithless followers, he was displaying the love for mankind of his heavenly Father. This is the meaning of the torn temple curtain. The breaking of Christ's body reveals the heart of God, the true Holy of Holies.

Mark 15: 33–39.

2 Sacrifice

The term most often used in the New Testament to refer to the death of Christ is the word 'blood'. From the earliest days of Jewish history, God's people were taught to offer animal sacrifices. The Writer to the Hebrews makes it plain that the blood of bulls and goats was not in itself capable of ridding men of the guilt of sin. But in an imperfect way these sacrifices pointed forward to Christ's sacrifice of himself, as the true and only way by which men may find forgiveness.

Hebrews 9: 6–14.

3 Propitiation

A propitiation is an offering to pacify someone's anger. Propitiatory sacrifices played (and still play) a large part in pagan religions, intended as they are to soothe the wrath of their deities against human sin. The Bible declares that God's anger is indeed aroused by sin. But what is distinctive about Christianity is the teaching that God himself has provided man with a propitiatory offering by sending his own Son to bear the brunt of human sin on the cross. Because Christ underwent punishment which he did not deserve, a repentant man may see this as God's way of offering him, without in any sense condoning his sin, free forgiveness.

Romans 3: 19–26.

4 Redemption

When the New Testament writers spoke of Christ's work on the cross as redemption, there were other pictures in their mind besides the sacrificial ideas which we have considered. One was the great interventions in history when God rescued the Hebrew people first from Egypt and then later from Babylon. Another was the legal ceremony in which a slave was freed on payment of a ransom-price. The point therefore is that by his death, Christ has delivered men from sin at tremendous cost, so that they may become the willing slaves of God.

1 Peter 1: 13–21.

5 Victory

To the eye of the passer-by, Christ's cruxifixion seemed like utter defeat. But when he was raised from the dead, the first Christians realized that far from being defeated, Christ had on the cross won a great victory over the powers of evil. Paul describes this victory as though Christ were a conquering Roman general, and as though the satanic forces had been paraded, like defeated enemies, through the streets.

Colossians 2: 8–15.

6 Example

In so far as Christ's death is to be understood as a sacrifice for sin or a victorious redemptive act, rescuing mankind and ultimately the entire universe from the powers of evil, his sufferings were perfectly sufficient and unique. But in so far as Christians are called to surrender their lives as a thank-offering to God, and in so far as they are sometimes treated unjustly when they seek to follow Christ, they have in him a perfect example. From first to last, Christ's life was wholly surrendered to God, and in his behaviour at death he showed the lengths to which undeserved sufferings must be patiently borne by those who seek his strength to bear them.

1 Peter 2: 18–25.

6 The Evidence for the Resurrection

1 The Empty Tomb

What is the evidence that Jesus Christ rose from the dead? The readings in this section are chosen to illustrate the converging lines of argument on which the Christian case is based. The first of these is that the tomb in which the most faithful disciples of Jesus expected to find his body was empty on the Sunday morning. If his friends had taken it, why did his closest followers not know? If his enemies had taken it, why did they not produce it to stifle the preaching of the Resurrection which filled the city a few weeks later?

John 19: 38—20: 9.

2 The Appearances to the Disciples

The second line of argument that Christ was raised from the dead is based on his appearances to the disciples. These have often been written off as hallucinations. But the weakness of this objection lies in the great variety of these recorded appearances. He appeared to them in many different places—in the garden by the tomb; in the upper room; by the sea; on the road to Emmaus. And he appeared to groups which differed from one another numerically, and consisted of people of varied psychological make-up.

1 Corinthians 15: 3–19.

3 The Scepticism of the Disciples

It is often suggested that the idea of Christ's resurrection arose from the wishful thinking of the disciples. But no

hint can be found in the Gospels that they took at all
seriously Christ's own prophecies that he would rise from
the dead. They did what they could to discourage him from
a course of action which they knew would lead to conflict
and death. When he was crucified they viewed it as a final
tragedy. The scepticism with which they greeted the first
news of the Resurrection, seen clearly in Thomas's reaction,
is important evidence that it really happened.

John 20: 24–31.

4 The Old Testament

One of the most important reasons why the apostles
became convinced of the truth of the Resurrection was the
stress which the risen Christ laid on the fact that it fulfilled
Old Testament Scripture. It was not a question of pointing
to a few isolated texts. The Resurrection provides the key
which unlocks the two great enigmas posed by the Old
Testament: how can God bring the tragic history of the
Jews to a destiny consistent with his power, justice, and
love? How can the Messiah be both a defeated servant and
a triumphant king?

Luke 24: 13–32.

5 The Transformation of the Disciples

When Jesus was arrested in the Garden of Gethsemane,
his disciples forsook him and fled. Six weeks later, they were
risking their lives to proclaim that though he had died on
the cross, he was alive. What could have changed them if
not the firm conviction that this message was true? But
human nature is notoriously hard to change, and the
Christian claim is that the transformation of the disciples
proves not only that they thought Christ had risen from the
dead, but that he really had. It is not easy to account for the
balanced strength and the dignified humility of their lives on
the view that they were victims of an illusion.

Acts 4: 1–22.

6 The Argument from the Nature of the Case

No *a priori* argument can count as historical evidence, and it is treacherously deceptive to try to decide, apart from historical evidence, what God is likely to have done or left undone. But the opponents of Christianity appeal shamelessly to such arguments: 'Miracles do not happen: why look at the evidence for the Resurrection?' If therefore a Christian asks for the argument from the nature of the case to be taken into consideration, it is simply to secure a fair hearing for the historical evidence, and not surreptitiously to add to it.

Acts 26: 1–29.

7 A letter to young Christians about the end of history

PAUL'S SECOND EPISTLE TO THE THESSALONIANS

1 New-found Faith

When Paul left Thessalonica on his first missionary journey, he felt that his mission there had been fruitless. He was so depressed by the sense of failure, that he began his work at Corinth only halfheartedly. Then news reached him that a flourishing church had taken root at Thessalonica after all. It had its problems. In his first letter to the Christians there, Paul had tried to deal with them. He wrote this second letter quite soon afterwards, when he gathered that the first had been misunderstood. But his thrill at their firm trust in Christ comes out clearly as he begins.

2 Thessalonians 1: 1–4.

2 The Danger of Unbelief

The infant churches were harassed by the same sort of persecution and unjust treatment at the hands of those who rejected the Gospel as was suffered by Paul himself. Far from being a mark of God's injustice, this fact would stand as crucial evidence, at the last day, of God's justice in counting Christians worthy of their reward. This leads the Apostle on to speak in strong terms of the danger of unbelief. But since he is writing to Christians, there is no question of his aiming to browbeat unbelievers into accepting his message through fear. His objective was to encourage the Thessalonians not to give up in face of persecution, and not to envy their persecutors, who were in a far from enviable position.

2 Thessalonians 1: 3–12.

3 The End of History: (a) the Power of Christ

Here we come to the heart of the letter. Paul had taught the Thessalonians about Christ's return during his original mission; he had enlarged on it in his first letter (4: 13—5: 11). But misunderstanding still prevailed, and he broaches the subject again. Some were insisting that the Return of Christ had already happened (and were even forging letters from Paul to this effect—see 2: 2; 3: 17): others had extravagant notions of the kind of behaviour required of them if it was imminent. A soundly based belief that Christ will come again should have the effect of giving poise and balance to a Christian's life.

2 Thessalonians 2: 1–12.

4 The End of History: (b) the Power of Evil

The tremendous strides taken in the 'Age of Reform', the period between the Napoleonic wars and the first world war, led a writer in 1912 rashly to predict that the millennium was already beginning to unfold. There is no suggestion in Scripture that history will gradually culminate in a golden age. There, all the evidence is that the end of history will be catastrophic, and, far from being heralded by growing peace and prosperity, it will be introduced by an unprecedented unleashing of the power of evil, involving the most serious trial for Christians alive to see the day, until Christ finally intervenes to set up his kingdom.

2 Thessalonians 2: 1–12.

5   Chosen from the Beginning

The odds against the possibility that anybody in Thessalonica would believe his message in the first place were so great that Paul had no hesitation in ascribing the conversion of those who did respond to the fact that God had chosen them. To be told that God had chosen them might have made them complacent. But Paul's purpose was far from encouraging them to sit back. It was, as always when he makes this point, to urge them to stand firm against the kind of opposition that they were facing— opposition of such intensity as to tempt them to suspect that God had abandoned them rather than chosen them.

2 Thessalonians 2: 13–17.

6   The Steadfastness of Christ

Preoccupation with their own theories of the Return of Christ had led many of the Christians at Thessalonica to take the attitude that there was nothing to be done but wait for God to intervene. They even abandoned any attempt to earn their own living. True faith, however, promotes not lethargy but urgent activity. Time is limited, but what there is must be profitably used. This is the note on which Paul's letter ends. The Christian is not to be an eccentric fanatic. He is to be a man who makes systematic and sensible use of all his opportunities, tirelessly pressing on, without being daunted by any discouragement.

2 Thessalonians 3: 1–18.